Our Amazing SUN

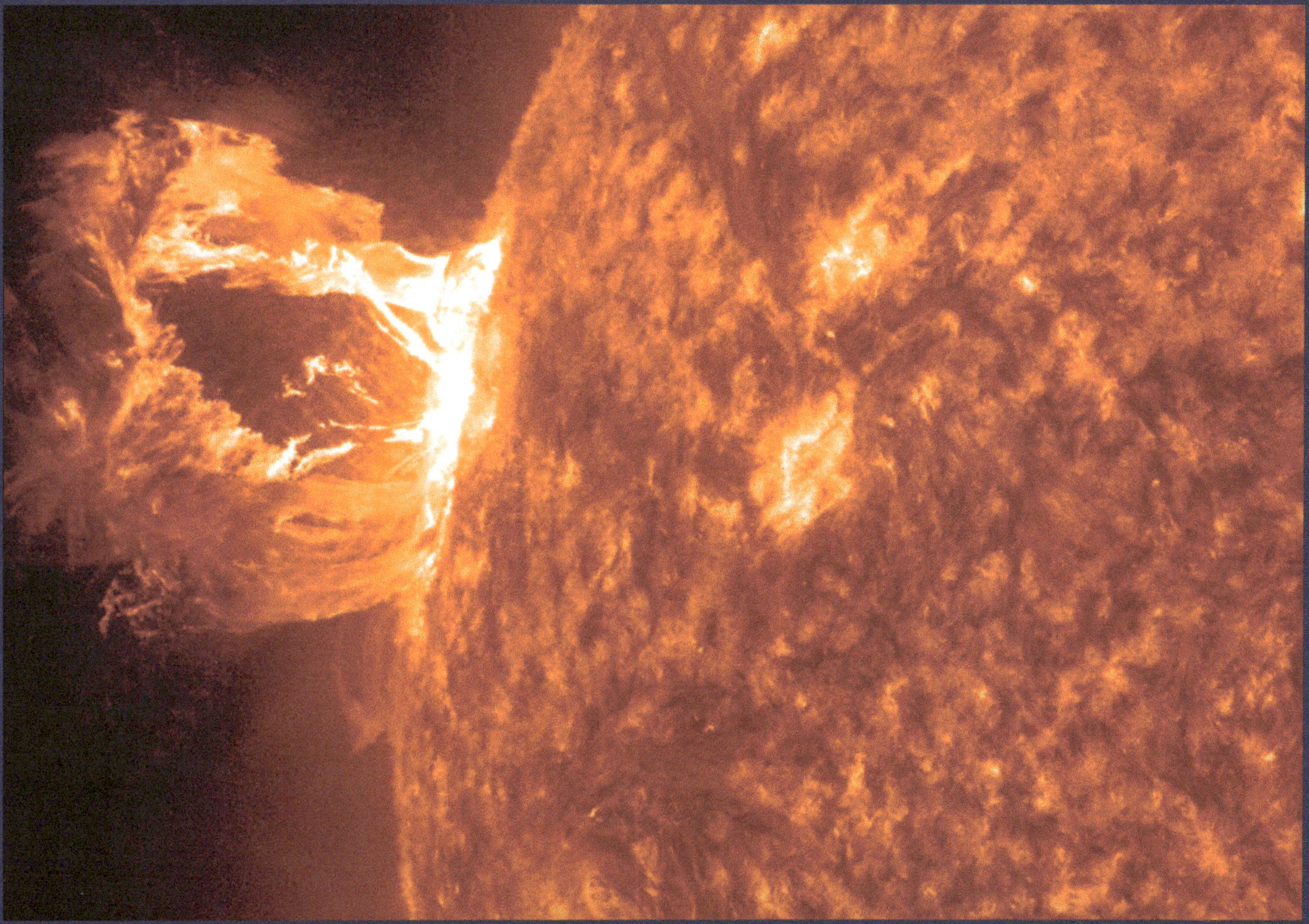

TJ Rob

Our Amazing Sun
By TJ Rob

Copyright Text TJ Rob, 2017
All rights reserved. No part of the book may be reproduced in any form without permission in writing from the author. Reviewers may quote brief passages in review.

Disclaimer
No part of this book may be reproduced in any form or by any means, mechanical or electronic, including photocopying or recording, or by an information storage and retrieval system, or transmitted by email without permission in writing from the publisher. This book is for entertainment purposes only. The views expressed are those of author alone.

Published by:
TJ Rob
Suite 609
440-10816 Macleod Trail SE
Calgary, AB T2J 5N8 www.TJRob.com

ISBN 978-1-988695-47-1

Photo Credits: Images used under license from Flickr.com, Pixabay.com, Public Domain, Wikimedia Commons:

Cover page, NASA Goddard Space Flight Center / Flickr.com; Back Page, AliceKeyStudio / Pixabay.com; pg. 1, NASA Goddard Space Flight Center /Flickr.com; pg. 2, WikiImages / Pixabay.com; pg. 3, WikiImages / Pixabay.com; pg. 4, Kevin Gill / Flikr.com; pg. 5, Public Domain via Wikimedia Commons; pg. 6, Siyavula Education / Flickr.com; pg. 7, Kelvinsong CC BY-SA 3.0 / Wikimedia Commons; pg. 8, Infographics / Pixabay.com; pg. 9, Infographics / Pixabay.com; pg. 10, WikiImages / Pixabay.com; pg. 11, WikiImages / Pixabay.com; pg. 13, WikiImages / Pixabay.com; pg. 14, Tablizer CC BY-SA 3.0 / Wikimedia Commons; pg. 15, Tablizer CC BY-SA 3.0 / Wikimedia Commons; pg. 16, Public Domain via Wikimedia Commons; pg. 17, NASA Goddard Space Flight Center / Public Domain; pg. 18, NASA Goddard Space Flight Center / Public Domain; pg. 19, NASA Goddard Space Flight Center / Public Domain; pg. 20, Unsplash / Pixabay.com; pg. 21, Skeeze / Pixabay.com; pg. 22, Kevin Gill / Flikr.com; pg. 23, At09kg CC BY-SA 4.0 / Wikimedia Commons; pg. 23, Qimono / Pixabay.com; pg. 24, The Odd Git / Public Domain via Wikimedia Commons; pg. 25, Siyavula Education / Flickr.com; pg. 26, eak_kkk / Pixabay.com; pg. 26, Amit Patel CC BY 2.0 / Wikimedia Commons; pg. 27, Skeeze / Pixabay.com; pg. 27, PIRO4D / Pixabay.com; pg. 28, Skeeze / Pixabay.com; pg. 29, Pexels / Pixabay.com; pg. 30, Infographics / Pixabay.com; pg. 31, Hinode XRT / Public Domain via Wikimedia Commons; pg. 31, Skeeze / Pixabay.com; pg. 32, NASA / Public Domain via Wikimedia Commons; pg. 33, NASA Johns Hopkins University Applied Physics Laboratory / Public Domain; pg. 34, NASA / Public Domain; pg. 35, NASA Goddard Space Flight Center / Flickr.com; pg. 35, NASA / Public Domain; pg. 36, NASA / Public Domain via Wikimedia Commons; pg. 37, NASA Goddard Space Flight Center / Flickr.com; pg. 38, Erik Axdahl Axda0002 CC BY-SA 2.5 / Wikimedia Commons; pg. 39, NASA Goddard Space Flight Center / Public Domain

TABLE OF CONTENTS

	Page
Why do we want to learn about the Sun?	4
What is the Sun?	6
What is the Sun made of?	7
How hot is the Sun?	8
How far is the Sun from Earth?	10
How big is the Sun compared to Earth?	11
How big is the Sun compared to other Suns?	12
How old is the Sun?	13
Will the Sun burn forever?	14
Does the Sun rise and set?	15
Does the Sun circle around something larger?	16
Fun Sun Facts	17
What is the Solar Wind?	18
How are the Auroras created?	20
What would life on Earth be without the Sun?	22
What does the Sun do for us?	23
What is a Solar Eclipse?	30
Solar Space Missions	32
Solar Wonders - Sunspots	35
Solar Wonders - Solar Flares	36
Solar Wonders - CME	37
Solar Wonders - Sun Dogs	38
More Fun Sun Facts	39
Please leave a review and Other EXCITING books by TJ Rob	40

Why do we want to learn about the Sun?

We look at the Sun rising every day. It's bright, it's big and it warms us up. Our Sun is the brightest object in our skies and naturally we are really curious to know more about it.

Our Sun gives us light, heat and energy. It may seem that energy comes from other sources such as gasoline and electricity but the ultimate source of energy for the Earth is nothing else but the Sun.

Without the Sun life on Earth would not exist. It would be so cold that no living thing would be able to survive and our planet would be completely frozen.

The Milky Way Galaxy

← Sun

The Sun is a star. Stars are all part of galaxies.

The Sun is much closer to us than any other star, and by studying the Sun, we can therefore learn more about other stars.

The better we understand other stars, the more we know about the Milky Way, the galaxy that Earth is part of.

From there we know more about other galaxies and in the end we learn more about the universe.

What is the Sun?

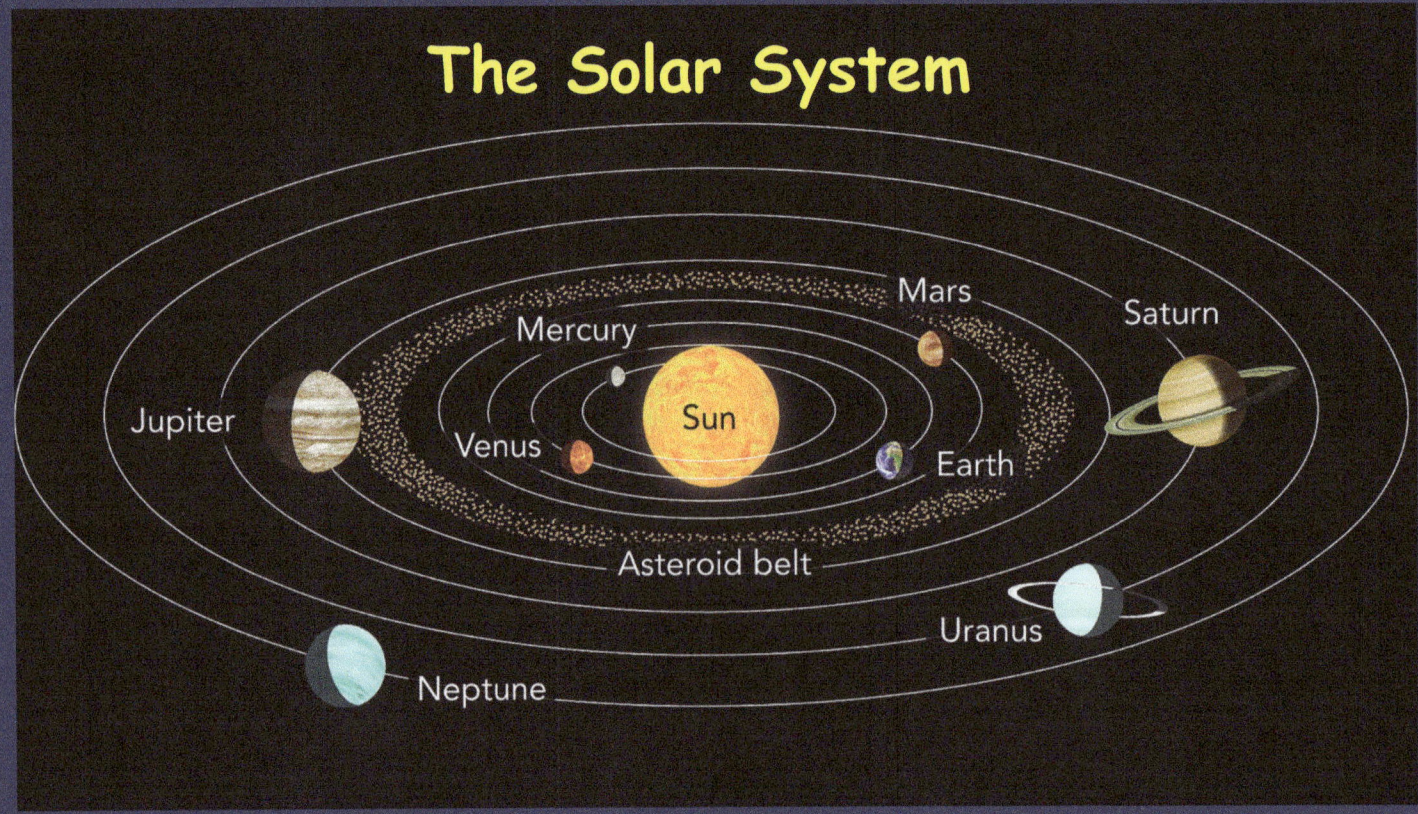

The Sun at the heart of our Solar System is a yellow dwarf star, a hot ball of glowing gases. The Sun plays the role of a big anchor, which creates gravity that keeps our planet and the other planets of the Solar System together.

All the planets in our Solar System orbit (circle around) the Sun.

If it weren't for the Sun, our planet would simply fly off into the Universe.

What is the Sun made of?

The Sun, like others stars, is a ball of gas. It is made of 91.0% hydrogen and 8.9% helium.

The Sun has six regions.

The first 3 make up the inner layers:
1. the Core
2. the Radiative Zone
3. the Convective Zone in the interior

The next 3 are the outer layers:
4. the visible surface, called the Photosphere
5. the Chromosphere
6. the outermost region, the Corona.

The Sun is held together by the force of gravity. It has huge pressure and temperature at the Core.

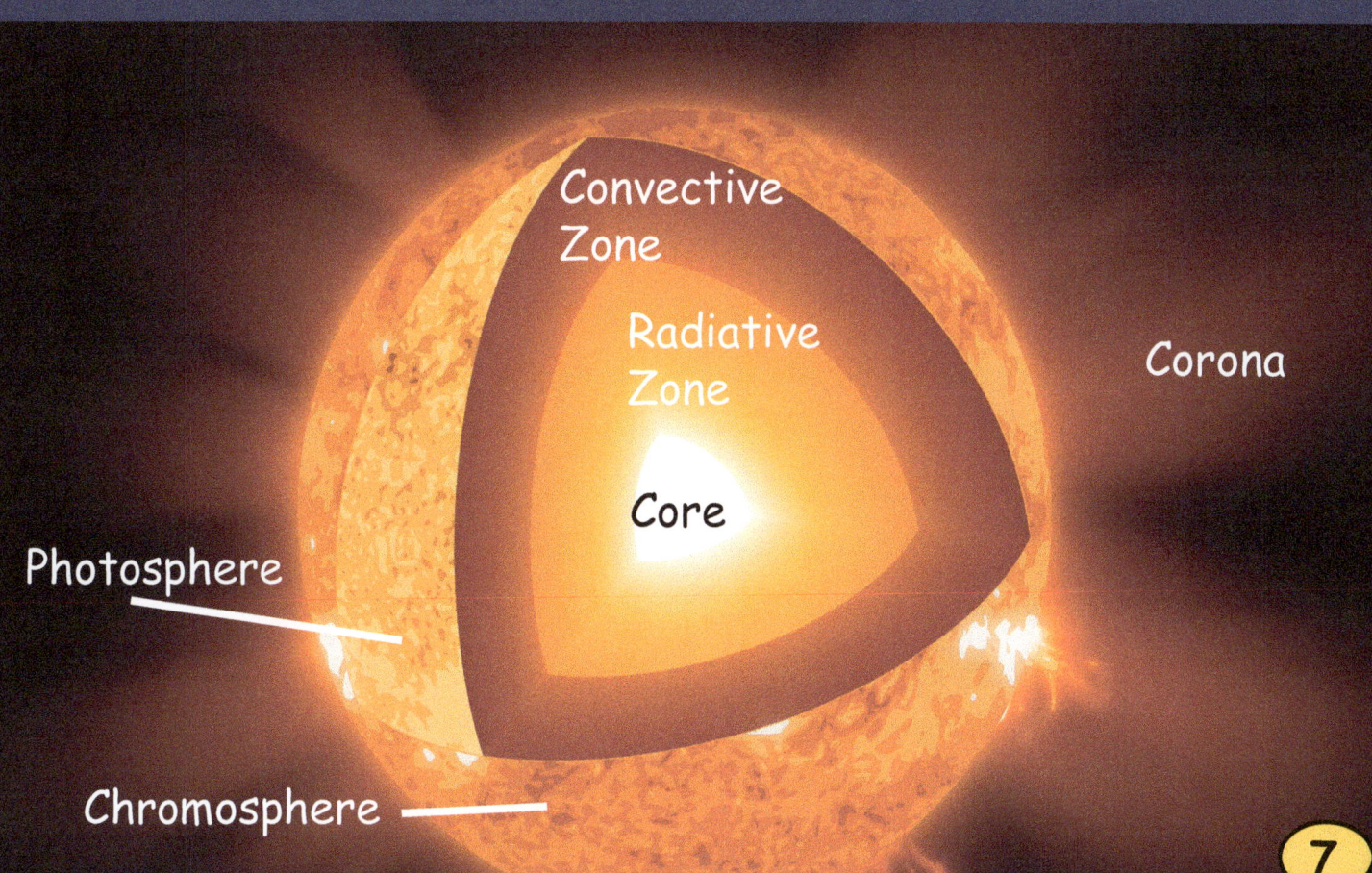

How hot is the Sun?

At the Core, the Sun's temperature is about 27 Million degrees Fahrenheit (15 million degrees Celsius). A process called Nuclear Fusion, takes place in the Core.

In the Sun's Core Hydrogen atoms fuse together to make Helium. During this process they release huge amounts of energy.

This is the same process that happens when we explode a nuclear bomb. Instead of one exploding bomb the Sun is like many huge nuclear bombs that explode without end.

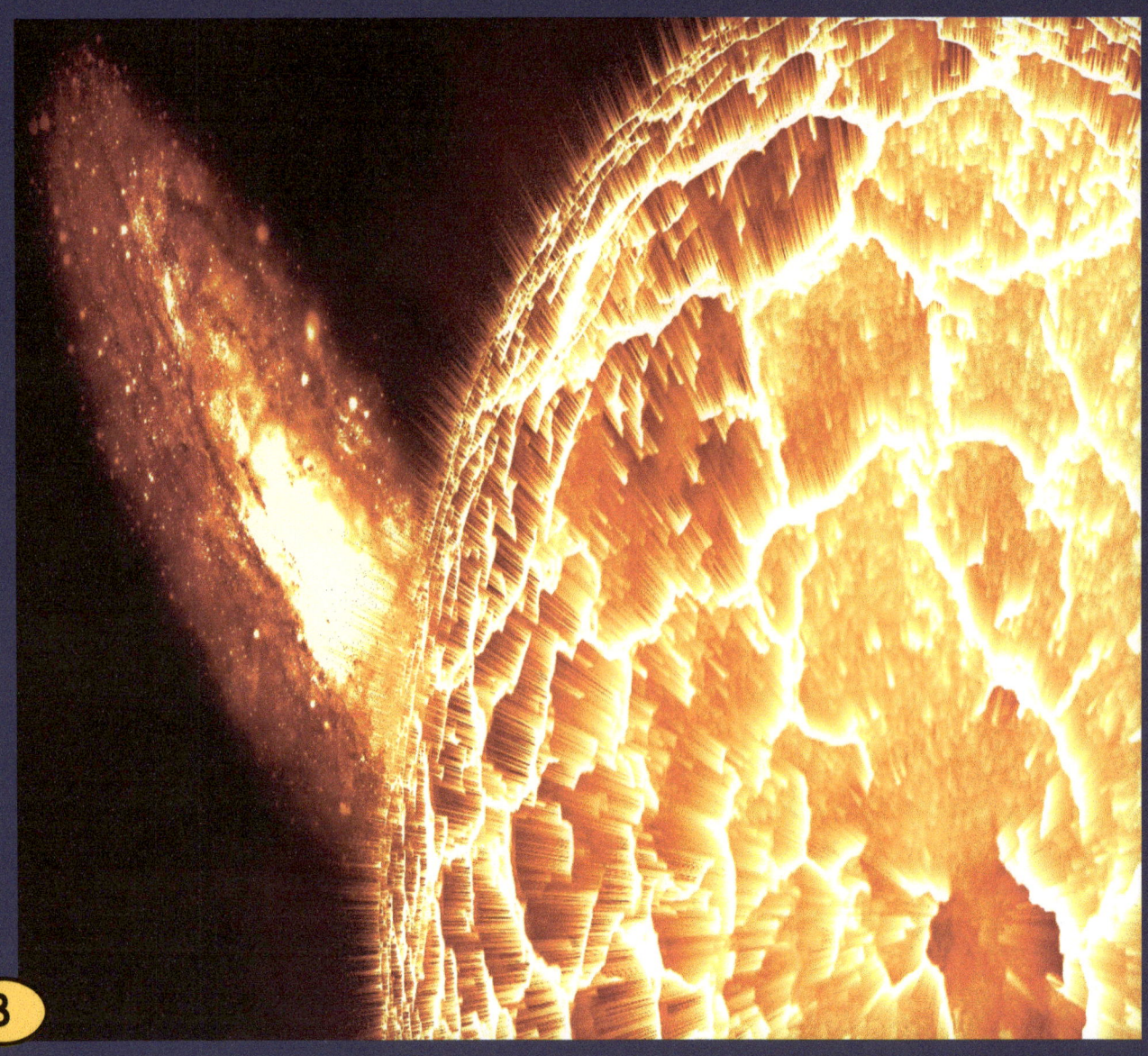

The energy produced in the Core powers the Sun and produces all the heat and light that the Sun gives off.

Energy from the Core is carried outward by Radiation.
It takes thousands of years for energy to get from the Core to the surface of the Sun.

The surface of the sun - the part we can see - is about 10,000 degrees Fahrenheit (5,500 degrees Celsius). That's much cooler than the blazing Core, but it's still hot enough to make diamonds not just melt, but boil.

How far is the Sun from Earth?

The Sun is at an average distance of 93 million miles (150 million kilometers) away from Earth. It is so far away that light from the Sun, traveling at a speed of 186,000 miles (300,000 kilometers) per second, takes about 8 minutes to reach us.

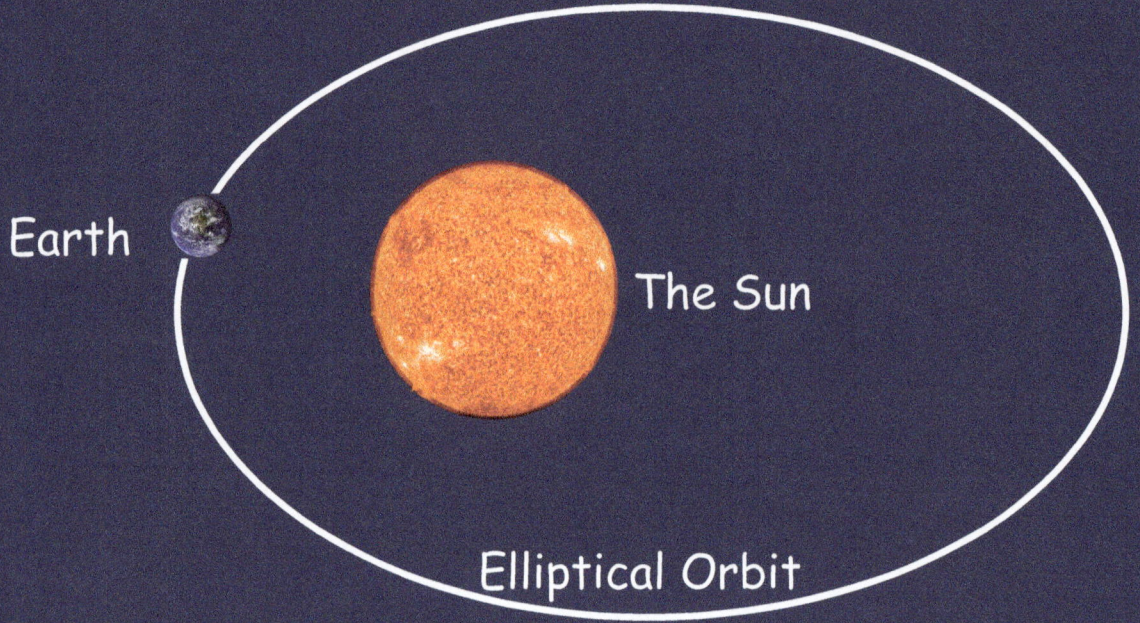

Like all of the other planets in our Solar System, Earth does not travel around the Sun in a perfect circle.

Instead its orbit is elliptical, like a stretched circle, with the Sun just off the center of the orbit.

This means that the distance between Earth and the Sun changes during a year.

At its closest, the Sun is 91.4 million miles (147.1 million km) away from us. At its farthest, the Sun is 94.5 million miles (152.1 million km) away.

How big is the Sun compared to Earth?

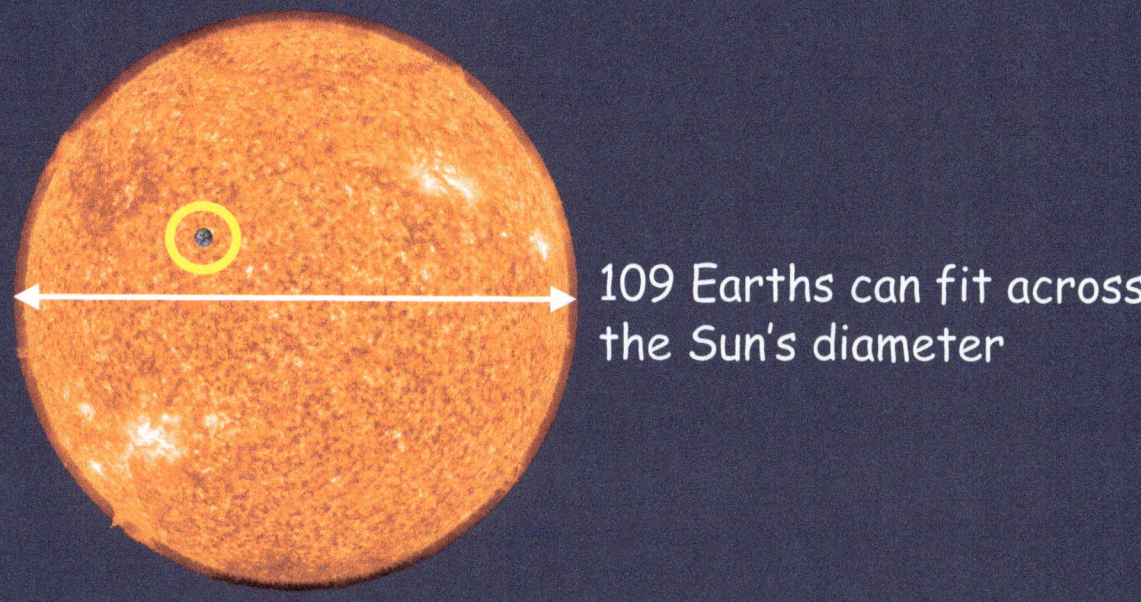

109 Earths can fit across the Sun's diameter

The Sun is 864,400 miles (1,391,000 kilometers) across.

This is about 109 times the diameter of Earth.

The Sun weighs about 333,000 times as much as Earth.

It is so large that about 1,3 million planet Earths can fit inside of it.

How big is the Sun compared to other suns?

Our Sun is an average sized star in the Milky Way Galaxy.

There are bigger stars, and there are smaller stars. There are enormous stars that are more than 100 times bigger in diameter than our Sun. We have also seen stars that are just one tenth the size of our Sun.

While the Sun might dwarf the Earth, it is tiny compared to some of the largest stars in our galaxy, the Milky Way.

The biggest star in the Milky Way Galaxy is VY Canis Majoris. This star has a diameter roughly 2000 times that of our Sun and 155,000 times that of Earth. VY Canis Majoris is located 3,900 light years from Earth. (1 light year is the speed that light would take to travel in 1 year.)

The Sun

VY Canis Majoris

(The biggest star in the Milky Way Galaxy)

How old is the Sun?

The Sun was born about 4.6 billion years ago.

Many scientists think the Sun and the rest of our Solar System formed from a giant, rotating cloud of gas and dust called a Solar Nebula.

A star being born out of a Solar Nebula

The Solar Nebula collapsed because of its gravity. It spun faster and flattened into a disk. Most of the material was pulled toward the center to form the Sun.

The Sun is about 300 degrees hotter and about 6% bigger than when it was first born.

Will the Sun burn forever?

Our Sun will not burn in the sky forever.

The Sun has another 4 or 5 billion years before it uses up its hydrogen nuclear fuel. When this happens its outer layers will expand turning it into a Red Giant star.

The Sun will remain a Red Giant for another 1 billion years, growing about 250 times in size.

Eventually all of the Sun's outer layers will be blown away, leaving behind just the collapsed cooler core. It will then be a White Dwarf star.

The Life Cycle of our Sun

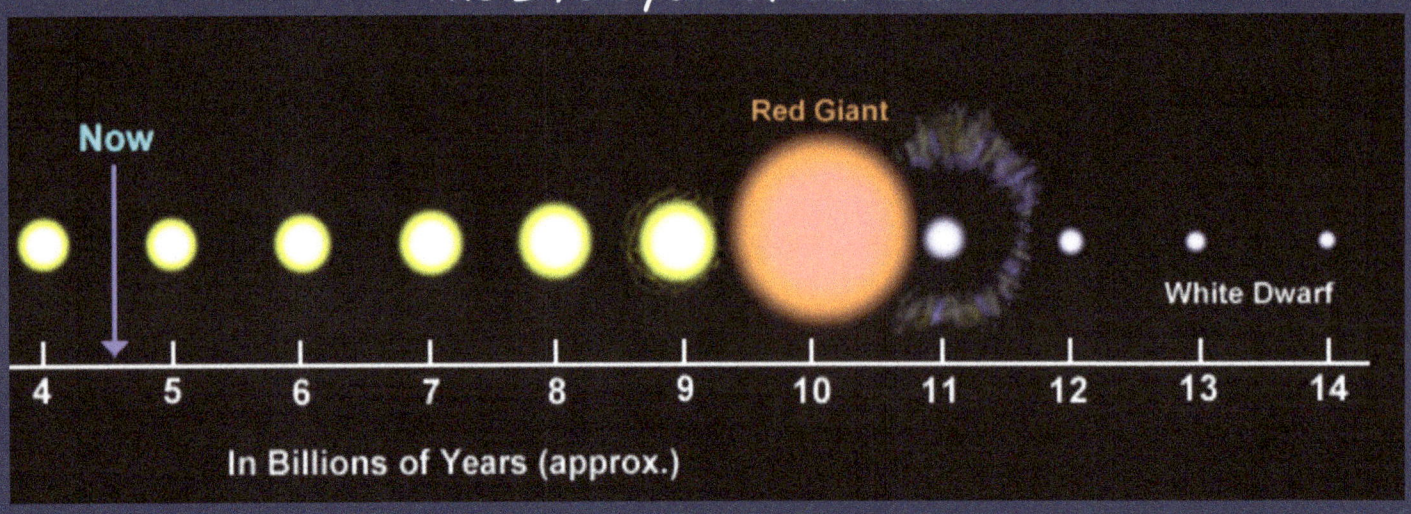

Does the Sun rise and set?

The Sun never sleeps. It keeps burning 24 hours a day, 365 days a year, every year... Here's what scientists say about "sunrise" and "sunset":

The Sun stays in its position at the center of our Solar System. It does not rise and set. But it appears to rise and set because of the Earth's rotation.

The Earth makes one complete turn every 24 hours - 1 full day. It turns or rotates toward the East.

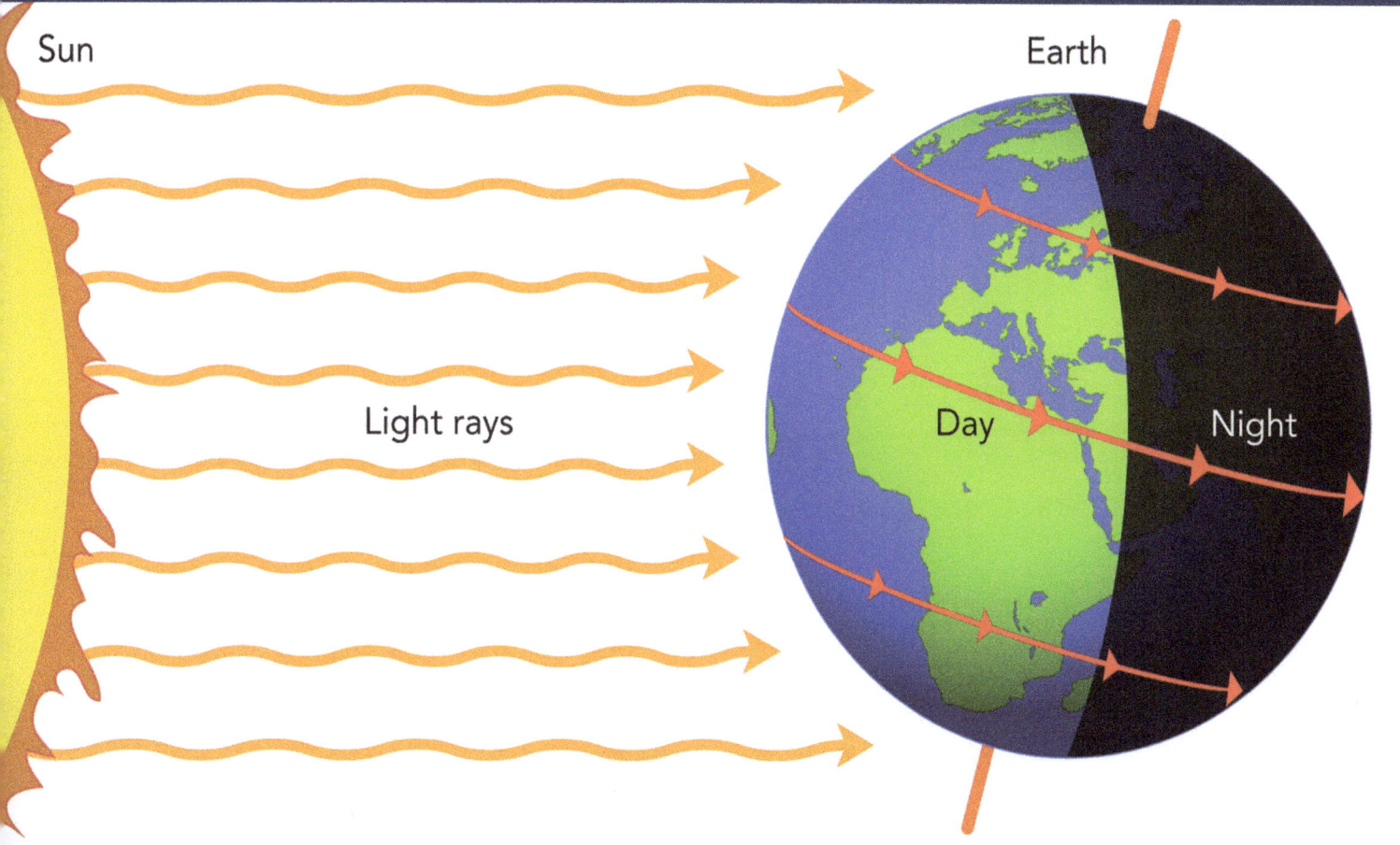

As the Earth rotates, different locations on Earth pass through the Sun's light.

As your city or town turns toward the Sun and begins to enter its light, the Sun seems to rise in the East. As your town begins to leave the Sun's light and enter darkness, it appears to set in the West.

Does the Sun circle around something larger?

The Sun is only one of many stars in our galaxy, the Milky Way.

It is located in one of the spiral arms about 30,000 light years from the Center.

It moves at a speed of 450,000 mph (720,000 km/h) in its orbit around the center of the Milky Way Galaxy.

The Sun takes roughly 250 million of our years to make one orbit of the Galaxy, known as 1 "Galactic Year".

Fun Sun Facts:

1. As orbiting passengers on Earth, we are all carried around the Sun at a speed of 66,600 mph (107,182 km/h).

2. Your eyes can get sunburned.

3. A bolt of lightning is 5 times hotter than the surface of the Sun.

4. The American flags placed on the Moon are now white due to radiation from the Sun.

5. The Earth's core is as hot as the Sun.

6. Looking at the Sun can trigger a sneeze in 10 to 35% of people.

7. If you weighed 150 lb (68 kg) on Earth, you would weigh 28 times as much on the Sun - 4,200 lb (1,905 kg).

What is the Solar Wind?

Electric currents in the Sun generate a magnetic field. A stream of electrically charged gas is constantly blowing outwards from the Sun in all directions. This is called Space Weather.

These gas particles are carried throughout the Solar System by the Solar Wind.

The Sun's outer atmosphere, the super-hot Corona, is the source of the Solar Wind. Though the Sun can lose more than 1 million tons of material every second, the amount is still tiny compared to the Sun's total mass.

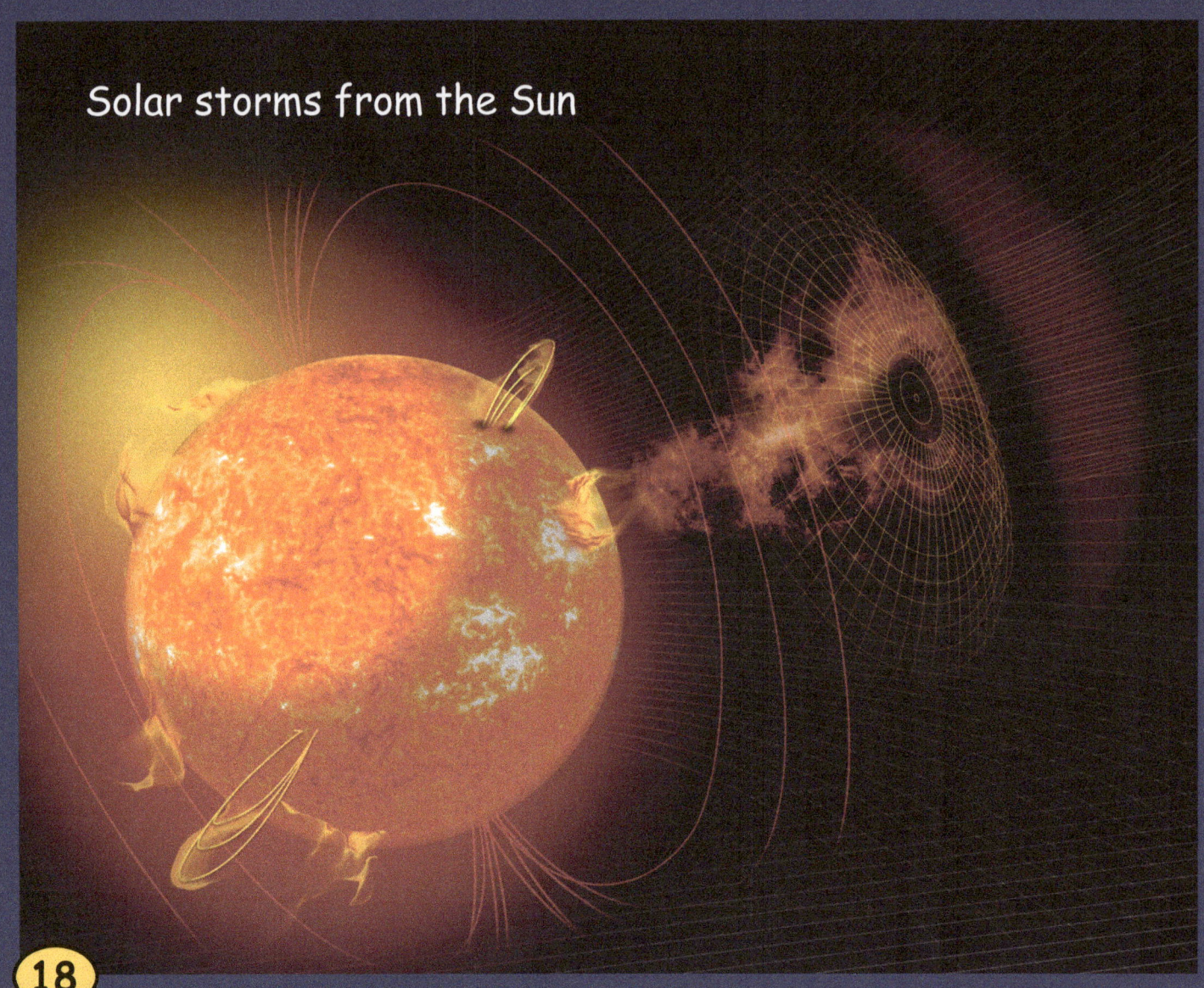

Solar storms from the Sun

The charged particles travel at more than 250 miles per hour (402 km/h) taking up to several days to get to the Earth from the Sun.

Earth's own magnetic field called the Magnetosphere protects our planet.

Because the Solar Wind is pressing on the magnetic field, the Earth's magnetic field is pushed in on the Sun-facing side.

On the side not facing the Sun, the Earth's magnetic field stretches out into a Magnetotail.

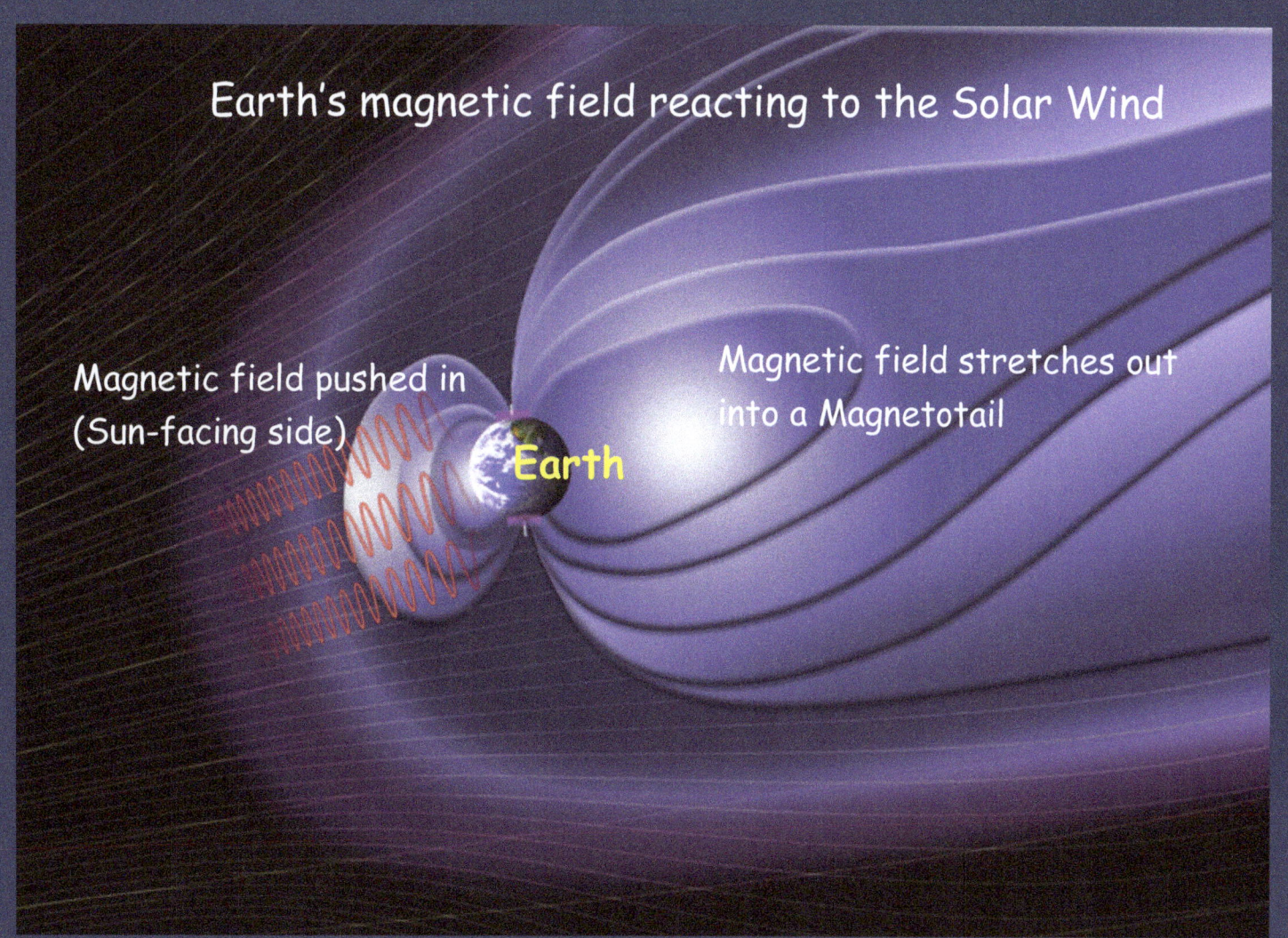

Earth's magnetic field reacting to the Solar Wind

Magnetic field pushed in (Sun-facing side)

Magnetic field stretches out into a Magnetotail

Earth

How are the Auroras created?

Occasionally, the Sun's charged particles find their way into Earth's Magnetosphere.

Those charged particles get sucked into the Earth's magnetic field and are then channeled toward the Earth's North and South Poles.

The charged particles hit the Earth's upper atmosphere to create the Northern Lights (Aurora Borealis) and the Southern Lights (Aurora Australis).

The Northern Lights seen above Earth from the International Space Station

The Northern Lights seen from Earth

What would life on Earth be without the Sun?

Without the Sun, all water on Earth would be frozen. Because the Earth is just the right distance from the Sun, its water is liquid.

Temperatures on Earth would be lower than -100 degrees F (- 73 degrees C).

The Earth would be in total darkness.

We would not be able to grow food.

Humans cannot survive on Earth without the Sun.

Without Sunlight, an icy, frozen Earth

What does the Sun do for us?

1. Photosynthesis

The Sun's energy helps plants to grow and produce their food through a process known as "photosynthesis".

Most animals on Earth eat either plants or other animals that eat plants.

This conversion of solar energy by the plants into food is how all of the plants and animals on Earth survive, including us humans.

2. Day and Night

The Sun provides us with light to see during the day. Without the Sun, the planet would be in complete darkness.

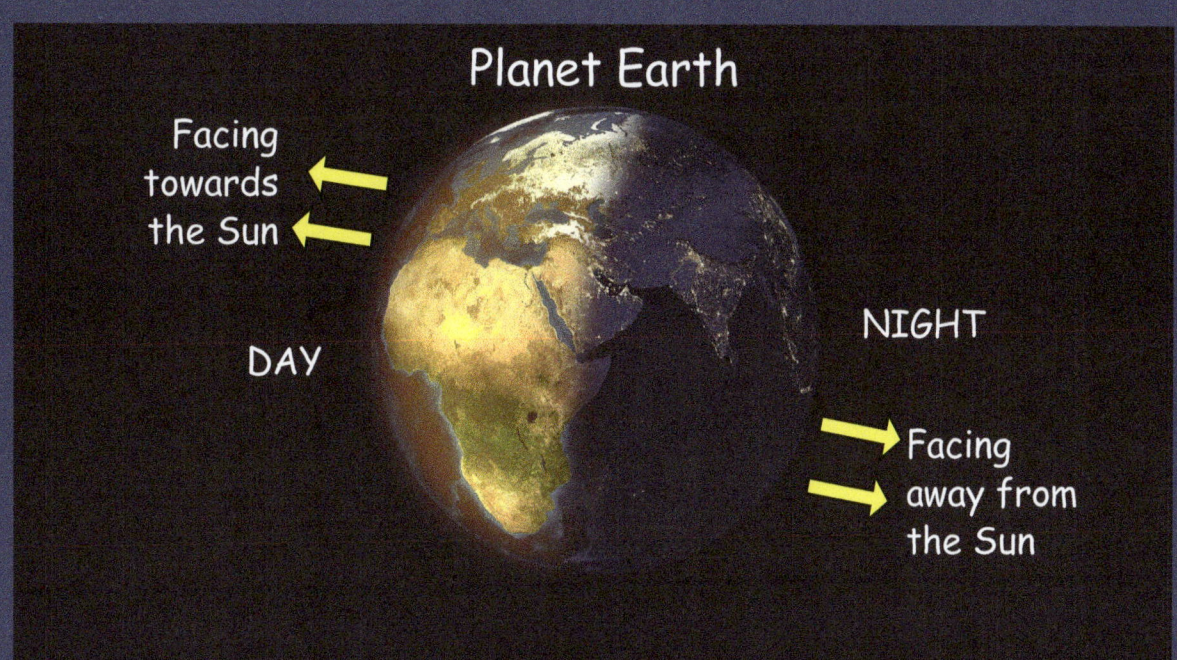

What does the Sun do for us?

3. Precipitation

The Sun heats and evaporates the water from oceans, lakes and rivers. The evaporated water is turned into steam and water vapor which then rises into the atmosphere in the form of clouds.

The wind moves the clouds.

From clouds we get precipitation like rain and snow.

If the Sun did not evaporate the water, there would be droughts and most of the world would be a barren desert.

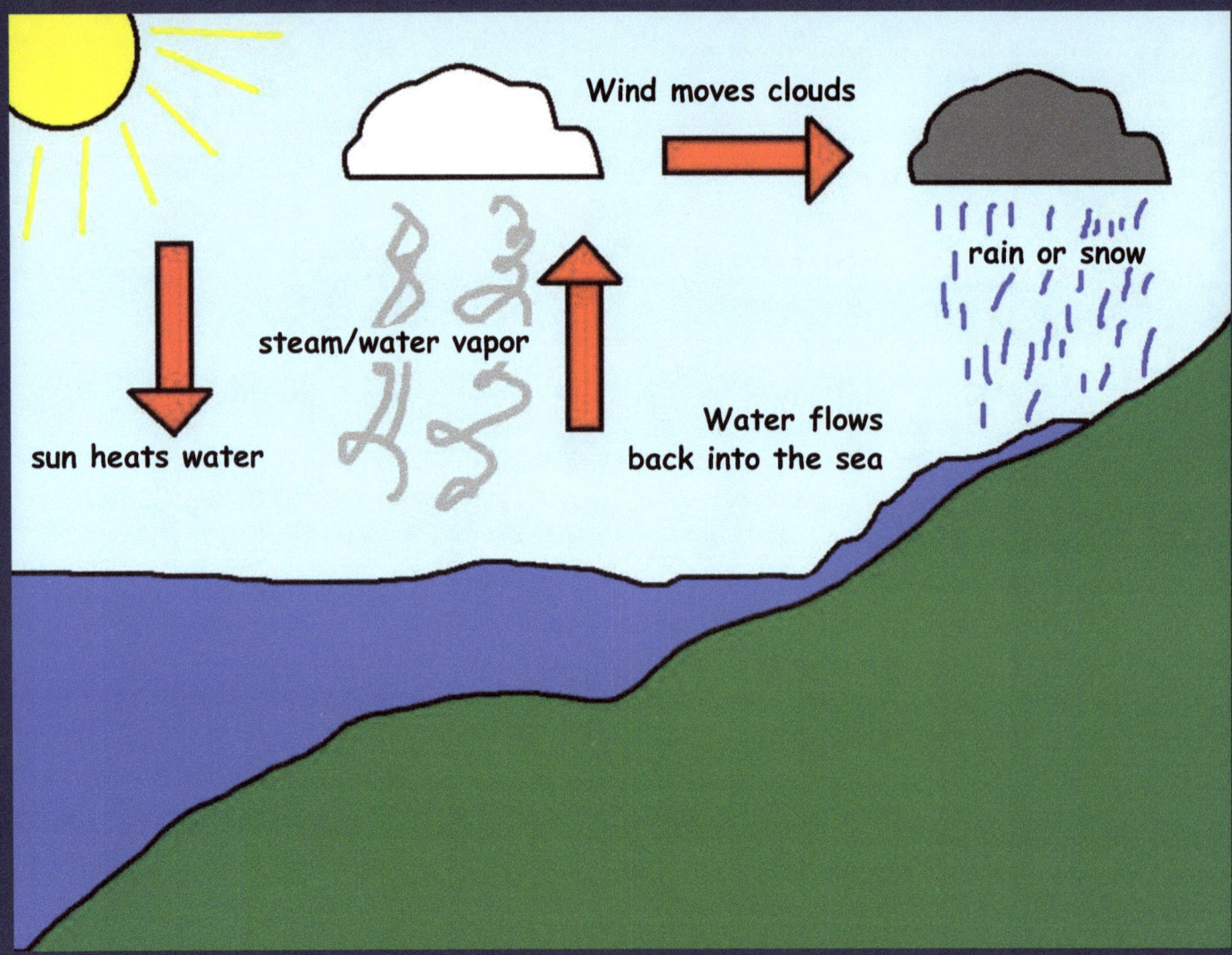

4. Produce Hydrocarbons

Sunlight is necessary to produce hydrocarbons such as coal and petroleum. Coal is fossilized plant matter, and petroleum is fossilized zooplankton and algae. The Sun helps break down the plant and animal matter using its heat. Over time the pressure breaks down the plant and animal material further and turns it into coal.

Modern society would not function well without hydrocarbons, such as coal for fuel in power stations and gasoline to power motor cars.

Even ancient people used the fossil fuels, animal fats, manure and wood made possible by sunlight to cook food and heat their homes.

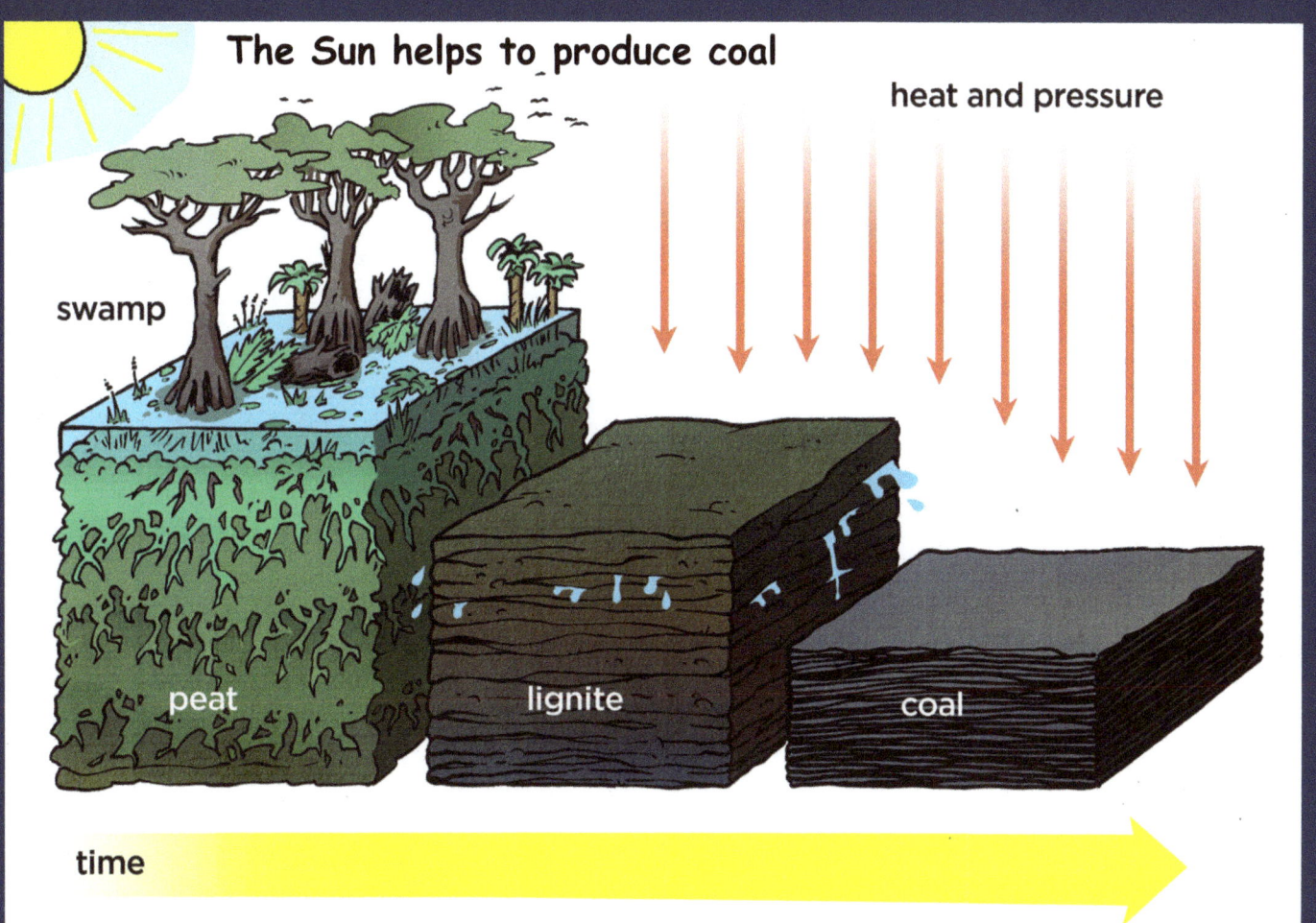

What does the Sun do for us?

5. Provides Power for Solar Cells

A Solar Cell is an electrical device that converts the energy of sunlight directly into electricity.

Watches and Calculators

Many watches and calculators have a tiny solar panel built into the watch face or the front of the calculator.

Sunlight hitting the solar panel charges the battery in the watch or calculator.

Solar powered watches

Solar Powered Stop Sign

Solar Panel →

Off-Grid Power for road signs

Instead of needing gasoline-powered generators many traffic, emergency and construction road signs use solar cells for power.

Rooftop Solar Panels

Many buildings and homes have solar panels that produce electricity. In most cases, the solar cells generate enough power to reduce the owner's electric bill from the local power utility company. The solar panel connects to a power management system that automatically switches to the power utility when solar power isn't available.

Rooftop Solar Panels

Satellites

Communications satellites need an electric power source that is lightweight, lasts for years, and works in outer space.

Because solar energy is abundant above the earth's atmosphere, solar power is the perfect solution for powering satellites in space.

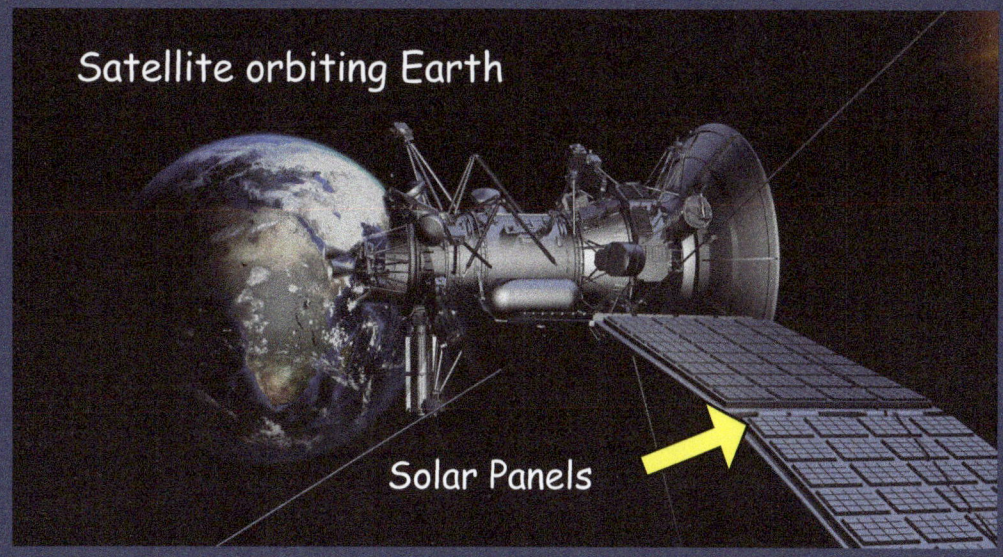
Satellite orbiting Earth
Solar Panels

What does the Sun do for us?

6. Solar Power Plants

Have you ever looked up on a hot day and said, "I wonder how much energy the Sun makes?" - Enough in 1 hour to power 2,880 trillion light bulbs.

This enormous amount of Sun energy is more than 35,000 times the amount of energy needed by everyone who uses electricity on Earth!

Solar power plants convert energy and heat from the Sun to provide electricity for homes and businesses.

Solar power is extremely clean, with no greenhouse gas emissions.

We are starting to make more of our electricity from solar power than ever before. Scientists predict that by 2050, more than one quarter of all our energy will come from the Sun.

The Array of Solar Panels at a Solar Plant

7. Vitamin D - Essential for us humans

One of the amazing things sunlight provides for us is Vitamin D.

Vitamin D is important for the creation and maintenance of bones. It helps the body use calcium and performs many other important jobs.

It is absorbed through the skin and converted to a state that the body can use.

Most people need 20 to 30 minutes of sunlight a day to get a minimum dose of vitamin D.

Are you getting your Vitamin D?

8. The Sun makes makes us feel HAPPY!

Many people find themselves feeling unhappy and depressed at the times of the year when there is less sunlight, like Winter. At these times of less sunlight some people who sit under sunlamps feel happier and more energized.

Getting some sunlight also helps with our sleep/wake cycles. It helps us have more restful sleep.

What is a Solar Eclipse?

A Solar Eclipse occurs when the Moon passes between the Sun and Earth. The Moon fully or partially blocks the Sun for a short period of time, normally lasting just a few minutes.

A Solar Eclipse can only take place at the phase of the new moon.

There are different types of Solar Eclipses.

A Total Eclipse:

With a Total Eclipse the Moon can appear to completely blot out the disk of the Sun. The Sun is completely covered. The Sun's Corona - the outer atmosphere of the Sun - is all that is showing.

Total Eclipses may last as long as 7 minutes 31 seconds, though most Total Eclipses are usually much shorter. On average a Total Eclipse occurs somewhere on Earth about every 18 months.

A Total Eclipse

Only the Sun's Corona is showing

An Annular Eclipse:

An Annular Eclipse is similar to a Total Eclipse in that the Moon appears to cover the middle part of the Sun.

The difference is the Moon is too small to cover the Sun completely. The sky will darken but not fully, because some of the Sun is still showing.

An Annular Eclipse

Part of the Sun is still showing

A Partial Eclipse

A Partial Eclipse:

A Partial Eclipse occurs when only a small part of the sun is covered by the Moon.

The Sun always remains in view during a Partial Eclipse.

How much of the Sun remains in view depends on the specific Partial Eclipse.

Solar Space Missions

There are 10 spacecraft observing the Sun currently. The following are some of the most famous spacecraft monitoring the Sun.

In 1995 a joint effort by both the National Aeronautics and Space Administration (NASA) and the European Space Agency (ESA), launched the Solar and Heliospheric Observatory (SOHO).

SOHO was designed to investigate the outer layer and interior structure of the Sun, and observe the Solar Wind.

SOHO has been observing the Sun since 1995, and sent back thousands of images.

SOHO

More recently, in October 2006, NASA launched the STEREO spacecraft.

This was actually two spacecraft.

These twin spacecraft were designed to watch the same activity on the Sun from two different angles, to give a 3-D perspective of the Sun's activity.

STEREO also helps astronomers predict Space Weather.

The twin STEREO Spacecraft

Solar Space Missions

The Solar Dynamics Observatory (SDO) is a NASA mission which has been observing the Sun since it was launched in 2010.

The SDO is taking a closer look at the Sun, the source of all Space Weather. Space Weather affects not only our lives here on Earth, but the Earth itself, and everything outside its atmosphere (astronauts and satellites out in space and even the other planets).

The SDO has been investigating how the Sun's magnetic field is generated and structured, and how this stored magnetic energy is converted and released into space.

The spacecraft is currently in a circular orbit at an altitude of 22,238 miles (35,789 kilometers) above Earth.

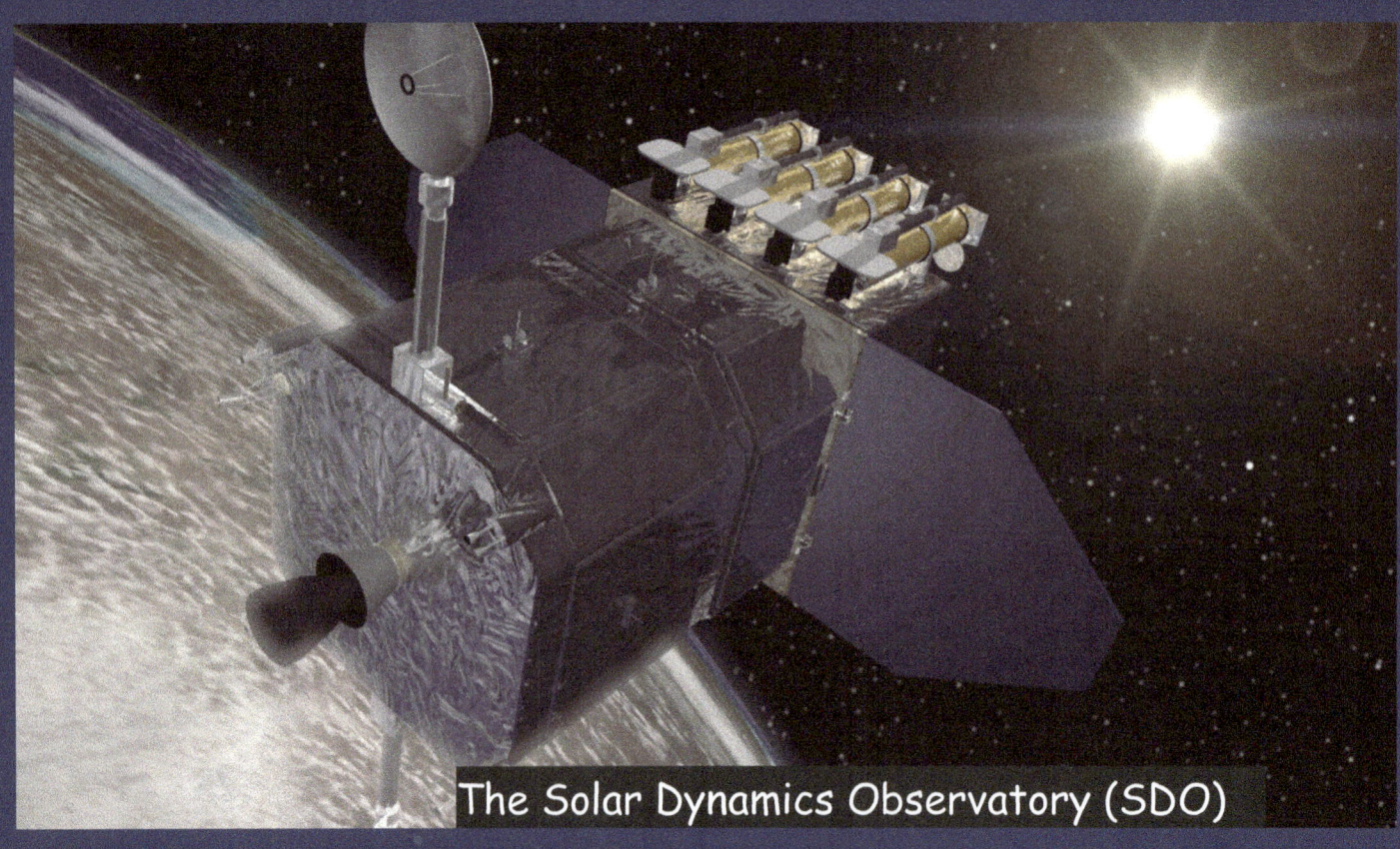

The Solar Dynamics Observatory (SDO)

Solar Wonders - Sunspots

Sunspots are temporary phenomena on the surface of the Sun that appear as dark spots compared to surrounding regions. They are areas of lower temperature. The Sun's surface has a temperature of 9980 degrees F (5535 degrees C). Sunspots have temperatures of about 6380 degrees F (3525 degrees C).

They look dark only in comparison with the brighter and hotter regions of the photosphere around them.

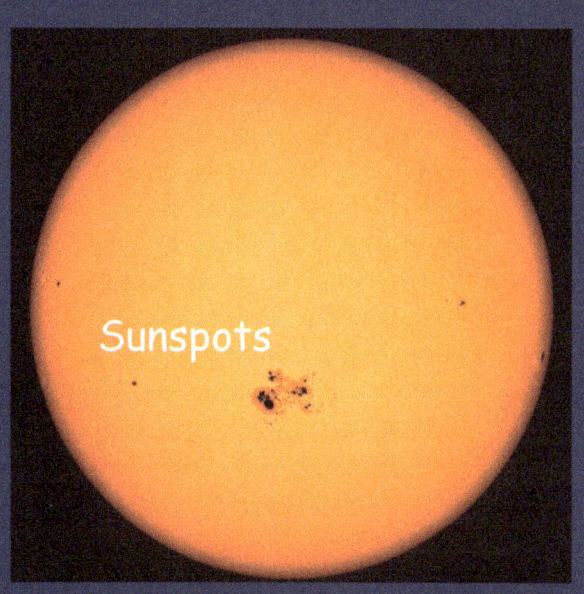
Sunspots

Sunspots close up

Individual sunspots may last anywhere from a few days to a few months, but eventually decay and disappear.

Sunspots expand and contract as they move across the surface of the Sun with sizes ranging from 10 miles (16 kilometers) to 100,000 miles (160,000 kilometers) across.

Larger Sunspots can be seen from from Earth without the aid of a telescope.

Solar Wonders - Solar Flares

Solar Flares are gigantic explosions of energy. A Solar Flare is a burst of x-rays and energy traveling from the Sun at the speed of light. Flares can last a few minutes to hours.

It takes 8 minutes for the light from a Solar Flare to reach Earth.

The heat of a Solar Flare can't make it all the way to Earth, but electromagnetic radiation and energetic particles can reach Earth.

Solar Flares can temporarily disrupt signal transmissions from an orbiting satellite to Earth.

A huge Solar Flare

tiny Planet Earth

Solar Wonders - CME

A Coronal Mass Ejection (CME) is a giant cloud of particles emitted from the Sun. A huge cloud of magnetized particles is hurled into space.

Traveling over 1 million miles per hour (1.6 million km/h), the hot material called plasma takes up to 3 days to reach Earth.

If Earth happens to be in the path of a CME, the charged particles can slam into our atmosphere, disrupt satellites in orbit and even cause them to fail. On Earth, a CME can disrupt telecommunications and navigation systems. It can affect power grids, and has been known to black out entire cities and even entire regions.

When these charged particles react with oxygen and nitrogen, they help create the Aurora, also known as the Northern and Southern Lights.

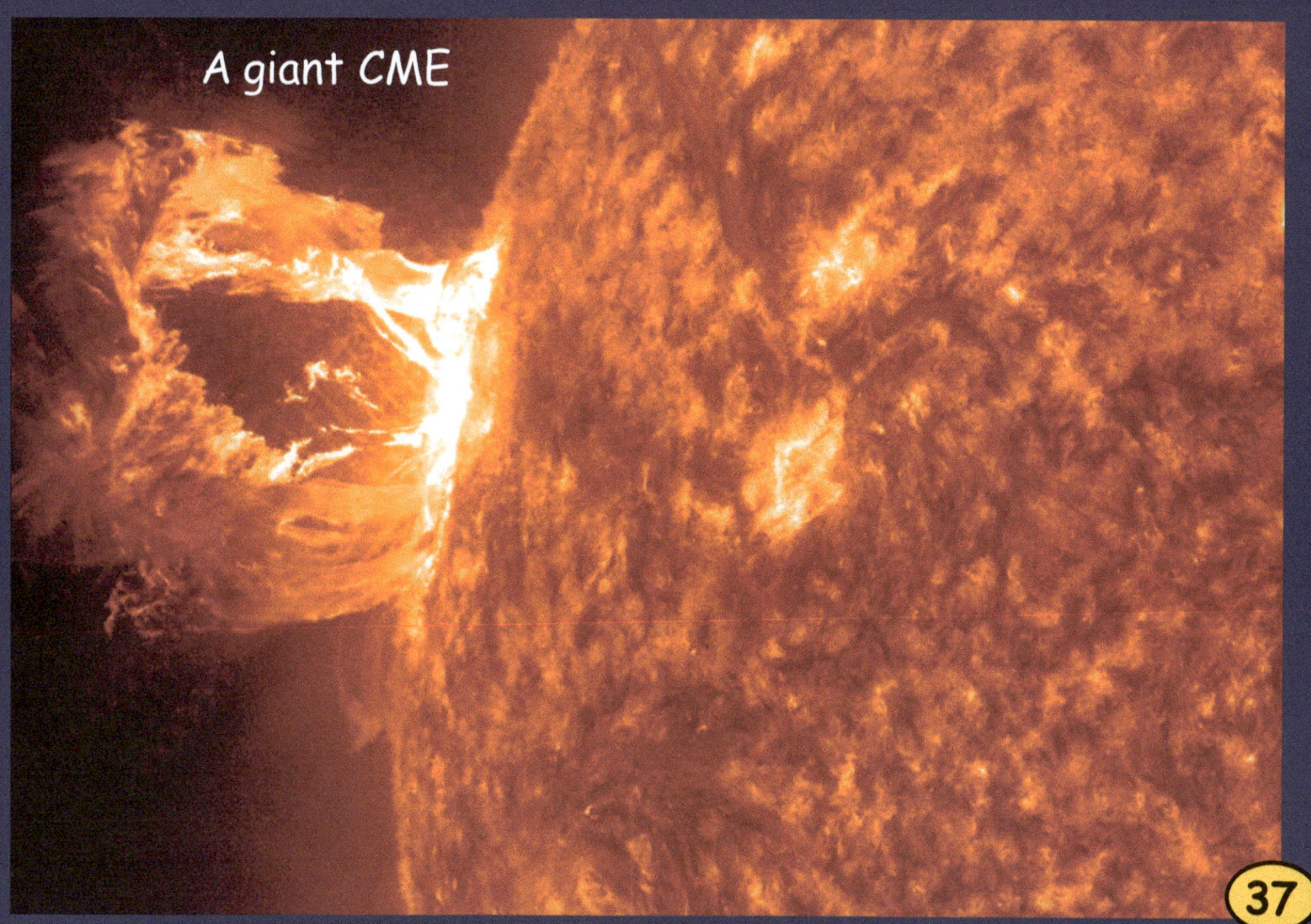

A giant CME

Solar Wonders - Sun Dogs

A Sun Dog, also called a mock sun or phantom sun consists of a bright spot to the left and/or right of the Sun.

Sun Dogs typically appear as two colored patches of light to the left and right of the Sun, at the same height in the sky as the Sun.

Sun Dogs are a type of halo, created by light interacting with ice crystals in the atmosphere.

They can be seen anywhere in the world during any season, but they are not always obvious or bright.

Sun Dogs are best seen when the Sun is close to the horizon.

Sun Dogs - Minnesota, USA

More Fun Sun Facts:

1. 100,000,000,000 tons of dynamite would have to be detonated every second to match the energy produced by the Sun.

2. Most ancient civilizations based their culture on the Sun. Many early cultures saw the Sun as a god. The Egyptians had a Sun god named Ra, the Aztecs had Tonatiuh, the Greeks had Helios, the Incas had Inti and the list goes on.

3. All planets orbit the Sun in the same direction, counterclockwise, and are roughly on the same plane, known as the Ecliptic.

4. The characters which make up Japan's name mean "sun origin" and its flag depicts the rising sun.

5. An area of the Sun's surface the size of a postage stamp shines with the power of 1,500,000 candles.

6. Every second the Sun gives off the same amount of energy as 10 billion nuclear bombs.

7. Most photos of the Sun depict it as being orange, red, yellow or a combination of the three. In reality, the Sun is white. It appears yellow to us because we see the Sun through the blue light in the Earth's atmosphere.

THANKS FOR READING!

Please leave a review at the website where you bought this book and tell others what you liked about it.

Visit www.TJRob.com to get a FREE eBook and to learn about other exciting books by TJ Rob:

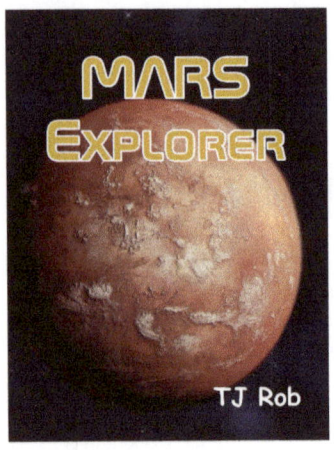

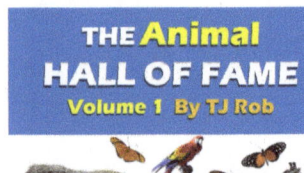

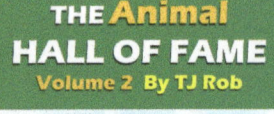

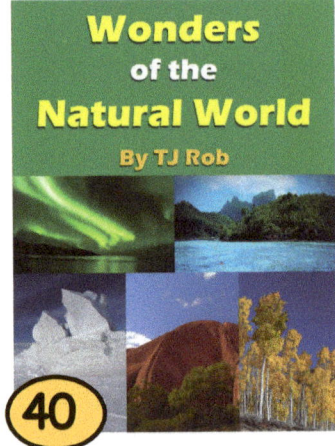
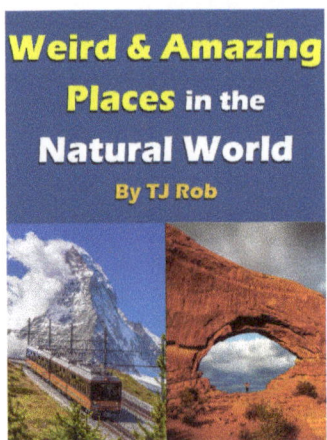
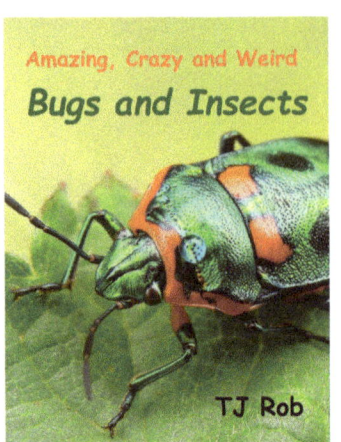
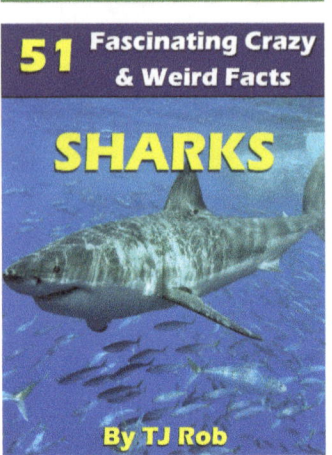